Holiday Histories

Earth Day

Mir Tamim Ansary

Heinemann Library
Chicago, Illinois

© 2002, 2006 Heinemann Library
a division of Reed Elsevier Inc.
Chicago, Illinois

Customer Service 888-454-2279

Visit our website at www.heinemannraintree.com

Designed by Kimberly Miracle and Q2A Creative
Printed in China by South China Printing Company

10 09 08
10 9 8 7 6 5 4 3

New edition ISBNs: 1-4034-8884-3 (hardcover)   978-1-4034-8884-8 (hardcover)
                           1-4034-8897-5 (paperback)   978-1-4034-8897-8 (paperback)

The Library of Congress has cataloged the first edition as follows:
Ansary, Mir Tamim.
    Earth Day / Mir Tamim Ansary.
        p. cm. -- (Holiday histories)
    Includes bibliographical references and index.
    ISBN 1-58810-220-3 (lib. bdg.)
    1. Earth Day – Juvenile literature. 2. Environmentalism – Juvenile literature. 3. Environmental
    protection – Juvenile literature. [1. Earth Day. 2. Environmental protection. 3. Holidays] I. Title.

GE195.5 .A57 2001
333.7 – dc21
                                    2001000070

Acknowledgments
The author and publishers are grateful to the following for permission to reproduce photographs: AP/Wide World p. 20; Bruce Coleman, Inc. pp. 18 (John Elk III), 28 (Steve L. Hilty); Corbis pp. 5B, 7, 19, 21, 22 (Ariel Skelley), 23; Getty Images pp. 26, 29 (Image Bank); The Granger Collection p. 9; Guy Palm pp. 4-5; North Wind Pictures p. 8; Photo Edit pp. 10 (Spencer Grant), 11 (Jeff Greenberg), 12-13 (Alan Oddie), 14 (Tony Freeman), 15 (Mark Richard), 16 (Spencer Grant), 17 (A Ramey), 24 (David Young-Wolff), 27 (David Barber); Tony Stone/ Getty p. 25; Underwood Photo Archives p. 6.

Cover photograph reproduced with permission of Kevin R. Morris/Corbis.

Every effort has been made to contact copyright holders of any material reproduced in this book. Any omissions will be rectified in subsequent printings if notice is given to the publisher.

Disclaimer
All the Internet addresses (URLs) given in this book were valid at the time of going to press. However, due to the dynamic nature of the Internet, some addresses may have changed, or sites may have changed or ceased to exist since publication. While the author and publisher regret any inconvenience this may cause readers, no responsibility for any such changes can be accepted by either the author or the publisher.

Contents

Some words are shown in bold, **like this**. You can find out what they mean by looking in the glossary.

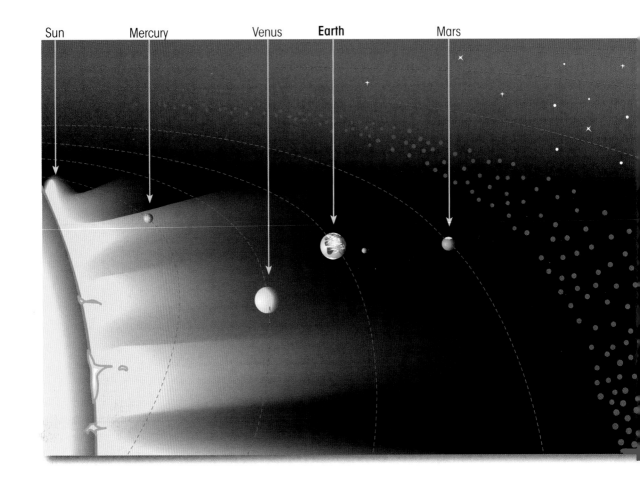

Sun   Mercury   Venus   **Earth**   Mars

Our Home Planet

Nine planets circle around our Sun. Each one is a ball of **matter** moving through space. The third planet closest to the Sun is our home planet, Earth.

April 22 is known as Earth Day. This is a day to celebrate our planet. It is also a day to think about its problems.

Before There Was Earth Day

When your grandparents were born, there was no such thing as Earth Day. Few people worried about Earth back then.

Most people thought they could never harm our planet. They thought our planet was too big to be harmed. People thought this for a long time.

More and More People

Thousands of years ago, there were not many people on Earth. They lived in tiny villages. The rest of the world was **wilderness**.

Over time Earth's **population** kept growing. People spread to most continents. More and more towns formed. Some towns became huge, crowded cities.

Machines Change Life

The growing **population** needed more and more food. In fact, people needed or wanted more **goods** of every kind. They invented machines to make goods faster.

To make more goods, people had to use more **resources**. They cut down more trees and dug up more metals. They used more of everything Earth provides.

The Pollution Problem

Fuels, such as **coal** and oil, made the new machines work. These fuels make harmful **wastes** as they burn. Such waste in the air is called air **pollution**.

The new machines also created water pollution. Harmful wastes came from factories, farms, and even homes. Pollution poured into streams, rivers, and lakes.

The Trash Problem

The more **goods** people used, the more trash they created. Getting rid of this trash became another problem. **Dumps** were filling up fast.

Nuclear power plants make electricity. They also make dangerous **wastes**. These wastes must be stored very carefully in special places.

Nuclear power plants give off steam that you can see, but they also make dangerous wastes that you cannot see.

Trouble for Animals

People began changing Earth to fit their needs. They drained swamps, cut down jungles, and dammed rivers. They changed the places where animals lived.

People are building their homes in **wilderness** places, harming the plants and animals around them.

Giant pandas are running out of habitat. They are in danger of dying out.

A habitat is the place where an animal lives. Many animals had trouble surviving once their habitats were gone. Some even became **extinct**.

Yellowstone became our first national park in 1872.

Worrying About Earth

In our country, some lands were made into parks. People were not allowed to live in these places or destroy them. But other places kept getting **polluted**.

In 1969 a river in Ohio got so polluted, it caught fire! By this time, many people knew the **environment** was in trouble. These people were worried.

Oil on the polluted Cuyahoga River in Ohio caught fire on June 22, 1969. Some flames were as high as a five-story building!

Earth Day Is Born

A man from Wisconsin, Gaylord Nelson, came up with the idea for Earth Day. He said there should be a special day to **honor** Earth. On April 22, 1970, the first Earth Day was celebrated.

Gaylord Nelson

That day about twenty million people around
the country took part in Earth Day activities. They
showed their concern for Earth. They marched
and gave speeches about how to help Earth.

Laws to Help Earth

Within two years of 1970, two new laws were passed. These laws made it harder for people to **pollute** air and water. Now some polluted places are being cleaned up.

Another important law was passed in 1973. It protects animals that are in danger of becoming **extinct**. It keeps their habitats from being destroyed.

These bald eagles are now protected by laws.

People Helping Earth

Some people are now helping Earth by **recycling**. They recycle glass, metal, paper, and plastic. Recycling helps save **resources**. It also creates less trash.

Cars make a lot of air **pollution**. Some people are trying to use cars less often. They get around on bicycles, buses, and trains when they can.

Science to the Rescue

Scientists are working on inventions to help Earth. A **hybrid car** is one such invention. It creates less air **pollution** as it runs.

Today electricity can be made from the sun and the wind. Someday wind and sunlight may replace **coal** and oil as **fuels**. Scientists are working on these ideas.

These windmills make electricity without making harmful **wastes**.

Our Planet's Future

What will our planet be like in the future? Will it be green and clean? Will it be gray and **polluted**? That depends on us.

Our actions will make the difference. Earth Day is a good time to think about the **environment**. What role will you play in the story of Planet Earth?

Important Dates

Earth Day

1794   The first **fuel** burning engine is invented

1800   The population in the city of London, England is one million

1872   Yellowstone becomes the world's first national park

1903   Pelican Island becomes the first safe place set aside for animals in the United States

1905   The United States Forest Service is established

1970   The first Earth Day is celebrated

1970   The Clean Air Act is signed into law

1972   The Clean Water Act is signed into law

1973   The **Endangered** Species Act is passed to help endangered animals

1995   The bald eagle comes off the list of endangered animals

Glossary

coal   black matter that is dug from the ground and used for fuel

dump   big hole in the ground where trash is buried

endangered   group of plants or animals that are in danger of dying out because there are so few

environment   world that surrounds us and affects how we live

extinct   group of plants or animals that has died out and can never live again

fuel   something that is burned to create energy

goods   things people use

honor   show respect for someone or something

hybrid car   car that uses less fuel to run

matter   what things are made up of

pollution   trash or noise that spoils a place and can hurt plants and animals. To create pollution is to pollute.

population   number of people in a place

recycling   using an item or material over again

resources   useful things found in or on Earth

waste   unwanted material left over after something is made or burned

wilderness   area not touched or changed by people

Find Out More

Galko, Francine. *Earth Friends at Home.* Chicago: Heinemann Library, 2004.

Gnojewski, Carol. *Earth Day Crafts.* Berkely Heights, NJ: Enslow, 2005.

Whitehouse, Patricia. *The Earth.* Chicago: Heinemann Library, 2004.

The United States Government Earth Portal
http://www.earthday.gov/kids.htm

Index